FILM QUOTES

Great lines from famous films

Compiled and edited by
John P. Fennell

Robinson Publishing
London

Robinson Publishing
11 Shepherd House
Shepherd Street
London W1Y 7LD

First published in the UK by Robinson Publishing 1991

A copy of the British Library Cataloguing in Publication
Data is available from the British Library
Printed in Great Britain

ISBN 1 83487 103X

CONTENTS

INTRODUCTION
THE TWENTIES 1
THE THIRTIES 5
THE FORTIES 39
THE FIFTIES 75
THE SIXTIES 103
THE SEVENTIES 133
THE EIGHTIES 157
THE NINETIES 183

This book is dedicated
to the late, great
HARRY BALL

INTRODUCTION

I am a film junkie. The lines in this book reflect my addiction. They are not intended to be, as Hollywood might hype them, 'The 501 Greatest quotes of All Time!' Rather, they reflect my personal favorites and they include most, if not all, of the best-known movie lines of our time. The six-plus decades of the 'talkies'–from 1927 through 1990–are represented roughly proportionately. The Thirties and Forties have more quotes than the Seventies and Eighties because so many more movies were made then. And while I recognize that quantity is no guarantee of quality, even a cursory glance at the lines from those early decades argues eloquently for their inclusion. As is apparent from my selections, I harbour a strong bias for certain movies made in 1939 and make no apology for the number of quotes included from that glorious year–they speak for themselves.

While researching this book I discovered that a number of my favorite movie lines were misquotes–or worse still, that they did not exist. Cary Grant, for example, never said, "Judy, Judy, Judy," and Charles Boyer somehow forgot to say, "Come with me to the Casbah." Neither Humphrey Bogart nor Ingrid Bergman actually asked Dooley Wilson to, "Play it *again*, Sam." Nor did Mae West say, in so many words, "Come up and see me sometime," or Gary Cooper drawl the exact phrase, "Smile when you say that." Saddest of all, I found that Jimmy Cagney never once snarled, "You dirty rat!" Yet these and other similarly jumbled lines continue to persist in filmgoers' imaginations and–well, who's to say they've done us any harm?

As films are the most democratic of all art forms, in that everybody feels free to summarily dismiss the verdict of any self-proclaimed 'expert' whose opinion might be contrary to their own, I welcome debate on the relative merits of any one line over any other. In the meantime, listen to what the film character Norma Desmond has to say about the advent of the 'talkies'.

> 'There was a time in this business when they had the eyes of the whole world. But that wasn't enough for them. Oh, no! They had to have the ears of the world too. So they opened their big mouths, and out came talk! Talk! Talk . . .!'

Gloria Swanson
SUNSET BOULEVARD, 1950

This book celebrates all those 'big mouth' actors and actresses, not to mention screenwriters, who have brought us so many years of enjoyment with their oh-so-quotable Talk! Talk! Talk!

I wish to extend acknowledgements and thanks to Janet Bailey, David DePolo, Ken Luboff, Marion and H. L. Scarborough, Jennifer Golden, my perspicacious step-daughters, Heather and Tatiana, and my film-loving sons, Morgan and Phineas. Harry Haun's encyclopedic *The Movie Quote Book* and Leslie Halliwell's monumental *Film Guide* were of immeasurable help as research aids. Thanks are also owed to my brother Tom Fennell for his research assistance and for being there when it counted. And to my wife Nancy I owe a special debt of gratitude, not only for her constant support, encouragement, and editorial assistance, but most of all because she falls for a good line when she hears one, every time.

 John F. Fennell San Francisco, California 1991

THE TWENTIES

"Yup!"
Gary Cooper's first (and frequent) line on screen
THE VIRGINIAN, 1929

"If you want to call me that, smile."
Gary Cooper to Walter Huston
THE VIRGINIAN, 1929

"Wait a minute, wait a minute, you ain't heard nothin' yet! Wait a minute, I tell you. You ain't heard nothin' yet! Do you want to hear 'Toot, Toot, Tootsie'?"

Al Jolson–first line in "talkies," in second reel of THE JAZZ SINGER, 1927

THE THIRTIES

"Gimme a visky with chincher ale on the side–and don't be stingy, baby."

Greta Garbo's first line on screen

ANNA CHRISTIE, 1930

"They call me Lola."

Marlene Dietrich to Emil Jannings

THE BLUE ANGEL, 1930

"One morning I shot an elephant in my pajamas. How he got into my pajamas I'll never know."

Groucho Marx

ANIMAL CRACKERS, 1930

"Another fine mess you've got us in, Ollie."

Stan Laurel and Oliver Hardy's frequent refrain

LAUREL & HARDY FILMS, 1930's

"You'll have to forgive me, Comrade."

Lew Ayres to the dead Raymond Griffith

ALL QUIET ON THE WESTERN FRONT, 1930

“Would you be shocked if I put on something more comfortable?”

Jean Harlow to Ben Lyon
HELL’S ANGELS, 1930

"Mother of Mercy, is this the end of Rico?"
Edward G. Robinson's dying words
LITTLE CAESAR, 1930

"Ay yam–Drak-ku-lah. . .Ay bid you velcome!"
Bela Lugosi to Dwight Frye
DRACULA, 1931

"It seemed like a good idea at the time."
Richard Barthelmess' oft-quoted line
THE LAST FLIGHT, 1931

"First the hunt, then the revels!"
Leslie Banks to his victim Joel McCrea
THE MOST DANGEROUS GAME, 1932

"I can't help myself!"
Peter Lorre
M, 1932

"We'll start with a few murders. Big men. Little men. Just to show we make no distinction."
Claude Rains's megalomania
THE INVISIBLE MAN, 1932

"It took more than one man to change my name to Shanghai Lily."
Marlene Dietrich to Clive Brook
SHANGHAI EXPRESS, 1932

"I am Mata Hari, my own master."
Greta Garbo
MATA HARI, 1932

"(Me) Tarzan. . .(You) Jane."
Johnny Weissmuller to Maureen O'Sullivan
TARZAN THE APE MAN, 1932

"What do you do?"

"I steal. . ."

Paul Muni's haunting fade out line
I AM A FUGITIVE FROM A CHAIN GANG, 1932

"I vant to be alone."
Greta Garbo to John Barrymore
GRAND HOTEL, 1932

"The white woman stays with me."
Warner Oland
SHANGHAI EXPRESS, 1932

"I'd love to kiss yuh, but I just washed mah ha-yer."
Bette Davis
CABIN IN THE COTTON, 1932

"Goodness, what beautiful diamonds!"

"Goodness had nothing to do with it, dearie."
Mae West to Cloakroom Girl
NIGHT AFTER NIGHT, 1932

"It went for a little walk. . ."
Bramwell Fletcher regarding the departed monster
THE MUMMY, 1932

"Am I a King or a breeding bull?"
Charles Laughton
THE PRIVATE LIFE OF HENRY VIII, 1933

"Beulah, peel me a grape."
Mae West to Gertrude Howard
I'M NO ANGEL, 1933

"It's not the men in my life, but the life in my men."
Mae West
I'M NO ANGEL, 1933

"Go out there and be so swell you'll make me hate you."
Bebe Daniels to Ruby Keeler
FORTY-SECOND STREET, 1933

"I was reading a book the other day. . .the guy said machinery is going to take the place of every profession."

"Oh, my dear, that's something you'll never have to worry about."
Jean Harlow and Marie Dressler
DINNER AT EIGHT, 1933

“Why don’t you come up sometime ’n see me. . .I’m home every evening.”

Mae West to Cary Grant

SHE DONE HIM WRONG, 1933

"Wa saba ani mako, O tar vey, Rama Kong."
(Translation: "The bride is here, O mighty one, great king.")
Witch Doctor presenting Fay Wray
KING KONG, 1933

"I suggest we give him ten years in Leavenworth or eleven years in Twelveworth."

"I tell you what I'll do. I'll take five and ten in Woolworth."

Groucho Marx and Chico Marx
DUCK SOUP, 1933

"Is that a gun in your pocket or are you just glad to see me?"
Mae West to Charles Osgood
SHE DONE HIM WRONG, 1933

". . .it was Beauty killed the Beast!"
Robert Armstrong's fade out line
KING KONG, 1933

"As long as they've got sidewalks, you've got a job."
Joan Blondell to Claire Dodd
FOOTLIGHT PARADE, 1933

"Box it."
Ned Sparks to Claudette Colbert
IMITATION OF LIFE, 1934

"Your wife is safe with Tonetti–he prefers spaghetti."
Eric Rhodes
THE GAY DIVORCEE, 1934

"You go. We belong dead."
Boris Karloff to Valerie Hobson
BRIDE OF FRANKENSTEIN, 1935

"We have ways of making men talk."
Douglass Dumbrille's oft-quoted line
LIVES OF THE BENGAL LANCERS, 1935

"If I'd have forgotten myself with that girl, I'd remember it."
Fred Astaire
TOP HAT, 1935

"The only fun I get is feeding the goldfish, and they only eat once a day!"
Bette Davis
BORDERTOWN, 1935

"I'll take my chances against the law. You'll take yours against the sea."
Clark Gable to Charles Laughton
MUTINY ON THE BOUNTY, 1935

"Hunger is an indulgence with these peasants as gout is with us."
Basil Rathbone's imfamous hiss line
TALE OF TWO CITIES, 1935

"Twas I informed on your son, Mrs. McPhillip. Forgive me."
Victor McLaglen to Una O'Connor
THE INFORMER, 1935

"Why, *everybody* in Mandrake Falls is pixilated–except us."

Margaret Seddon to Gary Cooper

MR. DEEDS GOES TO TOWN, 1936

"Too many girls follow the line of least resistance."

"Yeah, but a good line is hard to resist."

Helen Jerome Eddy and Mae West

KLONDIKE ANNIE, 1936

"I always look well when I'm near death."

Greta Garbo

CAMILLE, 1936

"Living, I'm worth nothing to her. But dead, I can buy her the tallest cathedrals, golden vineyards and dancing in the streets. One well-directed bullet will accomplish all that."

Leslie Howard to Humphrey Bogart

THE PETRIFIED FOREST, 1936

"Your dream prince, reporting for duty!"
Nelson Eddy (straight-faced) to Jeanette MacDonald
ROSE MARIE, 1936

"I can tell you what an Indian will do to you, but not a woman."

Gary Cooper's recurring problem
THE PLAINSMAN, 1937

"Now that you've got the mine, I'll bet you'll be a swell gold digger."

Stan Laurel to Rosina Lawrence
WAY OUT WEST, 1937

"If I see your eyes, I might forget to be a king."

Ronald Colman to Madeleine Carroll
THE PRISONER OF ZENDA, 1937

"The calla lilies are in bloom again. . ."

Katharine Hepburn's oft-repeated line
STAGE DOOR, 1937

"I'm sorry, Pepe. He thought you were going to escape."

"And so I have, my friend."

Joseph Calleia and the dying Charles Boyer
ALGIERS, 1938

"You've all suffered from their cruelty–the ear loppings, the beatings, the blindings and hot irons, the burning of our farms and homes, the mistreatment of our women. It's time to put an end to this!"

Errol Flynn rousing the peasants
THE ADVENTURES OF ROBIN HOOD, 1938

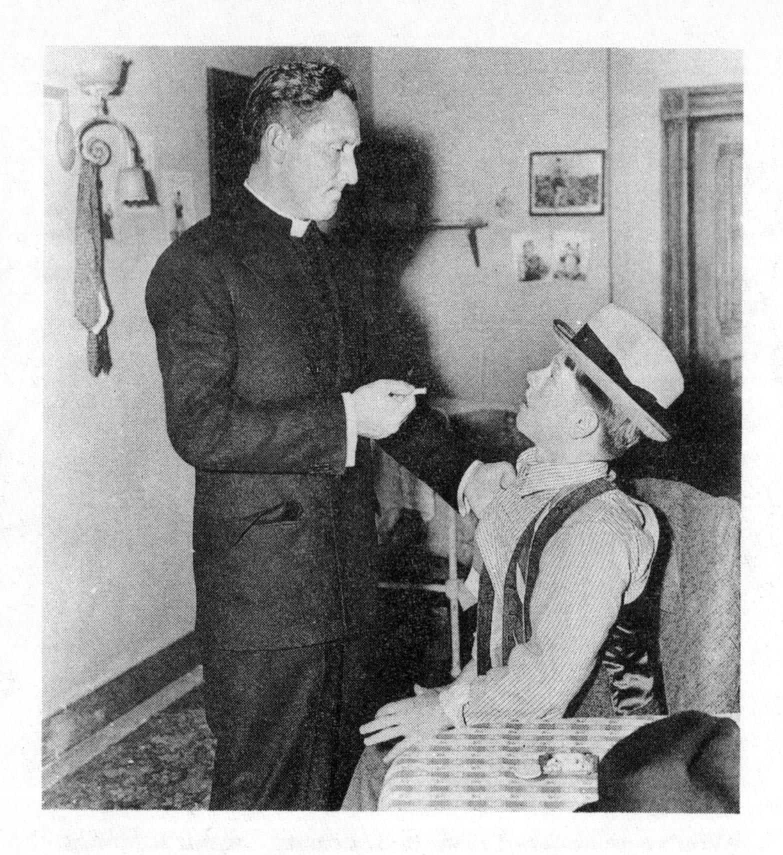

"Now, look, Whitey. In a pinch I can be tougher than you are, and I guess maybe this is the pinch. You're coming with me to Boys Town because that's the way your brother wants it and that's the way I want it."

Spencer Tracy to Mickey Rooney
BOYS TOWN, 1938

"I like my convictions undiluted, same as I do my bourbon."

George Brent

JEZEBEL, 1938

"Help me! I don't wanna die!"

Jimmy Cagney feigning fear

ANGELS WITH DIRTY FACES, 1938

"You're looking very regimental, Din."

Cary Grant to Sam Jaffe

GUNGA DIN, 1939

"Take him to the tower and teach him the error of false pride."

Eduardo Ciannelli to Victor McLaglen

GUNGA DIN, 1939

"See then down there, coiling and wiggling, sticking their pretty tongues out. . ."

Eduardo Ciannelli regarding snake pit

GUNGA DIN, 1939

"Toto, I have a feeling we're not in Kansas anymore."
Judy Garland in Oz
THE WIZARD OF OZ, 1939

"I'll get you, my pretty, and your little dog, too!"
Margaret Hamilton to Judy Garland
THE WIZARD OF OZ, 1939

"Pay no attention to the man behind the curtain. . .the. . . er. . .Great Oz has spoken!"
Frank Morgan to Judy Garland and friends
THE WIZARD OF OZ, 1939

"Toto, we're home. . .home. . .and this is my room, and you're all here. . .and I'm not going to leave here ever, ever again. . .because I love you all, and, oh, Aunt Em. . .there's *no* place like home!"
Judy Garland to all
THE WIZARD OF OZ, 1939

"Mad?. . .Mad?. . .Hannibal was mad, Caesar was mad, and Napoleon was surely the maddest of the lot!"

Eduardo Ciannelli to Victor McLaglen and Douglas Fairbanks, Jr.

GUNGA DIN, 1939

"As God is my witness–as God is my witness–they're not going to lick me! I'm going to live through this, and, when it's all over, I'll never be hungry again–no, nor any of my folks!–if I have to lie, steal, cheat or kill! As God is my witness, I'll never be hungry again."

Vivien Leigh
GONE WITH THE WIND, 1939

"Frankly, my dear, I don't give a damn!"

Clark Gable to Vivien Leigh
GONE WITH THE WIND, 1939

"Tara! Home! I'll go home, and I'll think of some way to get him back. After all, tomorrow is another day."

Vivien Leigh
GONE WITH THE WIND, 1939

"If only I had been made of stone, like you."

Charles Laughton to gargoyle
THE HUNCHBACK OF NOTRE DAME, 1939

"I don't know nothin' 'bout birthin' babies, Miss Scarlett."

Butterfly McQueen to Vivien Leigh

GONE WITH THE WIND, 1939

“That you, Martha?. . .I don’t want to be disturbed.”

Bette Davis’s dying words to Virginia Brissac

DARK VICTORY, 1939

“That was restful. . .again.”

Greta Garbo responding to Melvyn Douglas’s kiss

NINOTCHKA, 1939

“Don’t these big empty houses scare you?”

“Not me, I was in vaudeville.”

Nydia Westman and Bob Hope

THE CAT AND THE CANARY, 1939

“Somewhere, sometime, there may be the right bullet or the wrong bottle waiting for Josiah Boone. Why worry when or where?”

Thomas Mitchell

STAGECOACH, 1939

“Oh, Watson, the needle.”

Basil Rathbone to Nigel Bruce

THE HOUND OF THE BASKERVILLES, 1939

"I wouldn't give you two cents for all your fancy rules if, behind them, they didn't have a little bit of plain, ordinary, everyday kindness and a–a little looking out for the other fella, too."

Jimmy Stewart to Congress
MR. SMITH GOES TO WASHINGTON, 1939

"Are you eating a tomato, or is that your nose?"
Charlie McCarthy (Edgar Bergen's voice) to W. C. Fields
YOU CAN'T CHEAT AN HONEST MAN, 1939

"Take me to the window. Let me look at the moors with you once more, my darling. Once more."

Merle Oberon's dying words to Laurence Olivier

WUTHERING HEIGHTS, 1939

"She's got those eyes that run up and down men like a searchlight."

Dennis Moore about Joan Crawford
THE WOMEN, 1939

"Pity he had no children."

"Oh, but I have. Thousands of them. And all boys!"

Robert Donat rallying from his deathbed
GOODBYE MR. CHIPS, 1939

THE FORTIES

"What symmetrical digits!"

W. C. Fields regarding Mae West's fingers

MY LITTLE CHICKADEE, 1940

"There are but three things that men respect: the lash that descends, the yoke that breaks, and the sword that slays. By the power and terror of these you may rule the world."

Conrad Veidt infamous hiss line

THE THIEF OF BAGDAD, 1940

"Thank you, Mickey, and congratulations to you too."
Leopold Stokowski to Mickey Mouse
FANTASIA, 1940

"I'm Abu the Thief, son of Abu the Thief, grandson of Abu the Thief, most unfortunate of ten sons with a hunger that yearns day and night."
Sabu to John Justin
THE THIEF OF BAGDAD, 1940

"I'm asking you to marry me, you little fool."
Laurence Olivier to Joan Fontaine
REBECCA, 1940

"Ze roo-bies, Bella. . .give me ze roo-bies."
Anton Walbrook to Diana Wynyard
ANGEL STREET (U.K. title GASLIGHT), 1940

"I jes trying to get on without shovin' anybody, that's all."
Henry Fonda
THE GRAPES OF WRATH, 1940

"You're slipping, Red. I used to be frightened of that look–the withering glance of the goddess."

Cary Grant to Katharine Hepburn
THE PHILADELPHIA STORY, 1940

"Some day, when things are tough, maybe you can ask the boys to go in there and win just one for the Gipper."

Ronald Reagan to Pat O'Brien
KNUTE ROCKNE–ALL AMERICAN, 1940

"I'm not happy. . .I'm not happy at all."

Walter Abel's frequent refrain
ARISE MY LOVE, 1940

"Of all the fourteen-caret saps, starting out on a caper with a woman and a dog."

Humphrey Bogart saying it all to Ida Lupino
HIGH SIERRA, 1941

"See anything you like?"

Barbara Stanwyck to Henry Fonda
THE LADY EVE, 1941

"Yes, I killed him. And I'm glad, I tell you. Glad, glad, glad!"

Bette Davis laying it on thick
THE LETTER, 1941

"By *gad*, sir, you *are* a character!!"
Sydney Greenstreet to Humphrey Bogart
THE MALTESE FALCON, 1941

"What is it?"

"The stuff that dreams are made of. . ."
Ward Bond and Humphrey Bogart's fade out line
THE MALTESE FALCON, 1941

"A soul? A soul is nothing. Can you see it? Smell it? Touch it? No. . .!"

Walter Huston to James Craig
ALL THAT MONEY CAN BUY, 1941

"This is where we change cars, Alvin. The end of the line."

George Tobias's dying words to Gary Cooper
SERGEANT YORK, 1941

"I run a couple of newspapers. What do you do?"

Orson Welles to Dorothy Comingore
CITIZEN KANE, 1941

"I guess Rosebud is just a piece in a jigsaw puzzle. . .a missing piece."

William Alland's fade out line
CITIZEN KANE, 1941

"Hello, Monkey Face!"

Cary Grant to Joan Fontaine
SUSPICION, 1941

"She drove me to drink. That's the one thing I'm indebted to her for."

W. C. Fields

NEVER GIVE A SUCKER AN EVEN BREAK, 1941

"Where's the rest of me?"

Ronald Reagan to Ann Sheridan regarding missing limbs

KING'S ROW, 1941

"I guess you are sort of attractive in a corn-fed sort of way. You can find yourself a poor girl falling for you if–well, if you threw in a set of dishes."

Bette Davis to Richard Travis
THE MAN WHO CAME TO DINNER, 1941

"Yes, I love him, I love those hick shirts he wears and the boiled cuffs and the way he always has his vest buttoned wrong. He looks like a giraffe, and I love him. I love him because he's the kind of a guy who gets drunk on a glass of buttermilk, and I love the way he blushes right up over his ears. I love him because he doesn't know how to kiss–the jerk! I love him, Joe. That's what I'm trying to tell ya."

Barbara Stanwyck to Dana Andrews about Gary Cooper
BALL OF FIRE, 1941

"Mustard!"

Bette Davis to Jimmy Cagney
THE BRIDE CAME C.O.D., 1941

"You played it for her, you can play it for me. . .If she can stand it, I can– play it."

Humphrey Bogart to Dooley Wilson

CASABLANCA, 1942

"Here's lookin' at you, kid."

Humphrey Bogart to Ingrid Bergman

CASABLANCA, 1942

"I stick my neck out for nobody."

Humphrey Bogart's credo

CASABLANCA, 1942

"Chivalry is not only dead, it's decomposing."

Rudy Vallee

THE PALM BEACH STORY, 1942

"Why don't you get out of that wet coat and into a dry martini?"

Robert Benchley to Ginger Rogers

THE MAJOR & THE MINOR, 1942

“Play it, Sam. Play ‘As Time Goes By’!”
Ingrid Bergman to Dooley Wilson
CASABLANCA, 1942

"People all say that I've had a bad break, but today–today I consider myself the luckiest man on the face of the earth."

Gary Cooper to fans
THE PRIDE OF THE YANKEES, 1942

"My mother thanks you. My father thanks you. My sister thanks you. And I thank you."

Jimmy Cagney to adoring audience
YANKEE DOODLE DANDY, 1942

"Now for Australia and a crack at those Japs!"

Errol Flynn's fade out line

DESPERATE JOURNEY, 1942

"This is the people's war! It is our war! We are the fighters! Fight it, then! Fight it with all that is in us! And God defend the right!"

Henry Wilcoxon's film-ending sermon

MRS. MINIVER, 1942

"So they call me Concentration Camp Erhardt?"

Sig Ruman & Jack Benny's frequent refrain

TO BE OR NOT TO BE, 1942

"This is the screwiest picture I was ever in."

Camel to camera

ROAD TO MOROCCO, 1942

"You can't hurt me. I always wear a bullet-proof vest around the studio."

Elisha Cook's fade out (punch) line

HELLZAPOPPIN, 1942

"Your mother can't be with you anymore."
The Great Prince bringing the bad news to Bambi
BAMBI, 1942

"Yes, I killed him. I killed him for money and for a woman. I didn't get the money, and I didn't get the woman. Pretty, isn't it?"

Fred MacMurray confessing into dictaphone

DOUBLE INDEMNITY, 1944

"I've found peace in loving you. You shall have your house in Thornton Square."

Charles Boyer to Ingrid Bergman

GASLIGHT, 1944

"When I finish with my work, I wants my solitude and I wants my privitation."

Hattie McDaniel to Claudette Colbert

SINCE YOU WENT AWAY, 1944

"I don't know how to kiss, or I would kiss you. Where do the noses go?"

Ingrid Bergman to Gary Cooper

FOR WHOM THE BELL TOLLS, 1943

"Why don't you get a divorce and settle down?"

Oscar Levant to Joan Crawford

HUMORESQUE, 1944

"I can recommend the bait. I ought to know–I bit on it myself."

Tallulah Bankhead offering her diamonds for bait

LIFEBOAT, 1944

"You know how to whistle, don't you, Steve? Just put your lips together and blow."

Lauren Bacall to Humphrey Bogart
TO HAVE AND HAVE NOT, 1944

"Insanity runs in my family. It practically gallops."

Cary Grant to Priscilla Lane

ARSENIC AND OLD LACE, 1944

"Do you have a wee drop of the crature, about?"

Bing Crosby to Barry Fitzgerald
GOING MY WAY, 1944

"It's lavish, but I call it home."

Clifton Webb to Dana Andrews
LAURA, 1944

"Personally, Veda's convinced me that alligators have the right idea. They eat their young."

Eve Arden to Joan Crawford
MILDRED PIERCE, 1945

"Frederic, you must stop this Polonaise jangle!"

Merle Oberon to the tubercular Frederic Chopin, Cornel Wilde
A SONG TO REMEMBER, 1945

"Very stupid to kill the only servant in the house. Now we don't even know where to find the marmalade."

Judith Anderson
AND THEN THERE WERE NONE, 1945

"Did anyone ever tell you that you have a dishonest face–for a priest, I mean?"

Ingrid Bergman to Bing Crosby
THE BELLS OF ST. MARY'S, 1945

“What I’m trying to say is, I’m not a drinker–I’m a drunk.”
Ray Milland to Jane Wyman
THE LOST WEEKEND, 1945

"Ma'am, I sure like that name–Clementine."
Henry Fonda's last line to Linda Darnell
MY DARLING CLEMENTINE, 1946

"Tell me why it is that every man who seems attractive these days is either married or barred on a technicality."
Celeste Holm
GENTLEMAN'S AGREEMENT, 1946

"Alex, will you come in please? I wish to talk to you."
Ivan Triesault's ominous last words to Claude Rains
NOTORIOUS, 1946

"Pearl, you're curved in the flesh of temptation. Resistance is going to be a darn sight harder for you than for females protected by the shape of sows."
Walter Huston to Jennifer Jones
DUEL IN THE SUN, 1946

"You know, I've never been able to understand why, when there's so much space in the world, people should deliberately choose to live in the Middle West."
Clifton Webb
THE RAZOR'S EDGE, 1946

"We are protected by the enormity of your stupidity."
Madame Konstantine to Claude Rains
NOTORIOUS, 1946

"I hate the dawn. The grass always looks as though it's been left out all night."

Clifton Webb

THE DARK CORNER, 1946

"Get me back. Get me back. I don't care what happens to me. Get me back to my wife and kids. Help me, Clarence. Please! Please! I wanna live again. I wanna live again! I wanna live again! Please, God, let me live again!"

Jimmy Stewart to Henry Travers

IT'S A WONDERFUL LIFE, 1946

"Speaking of horses. . .You've got a touch of class, but I don't know how–how far you can go."

"A lot depends on who's in the saddle."

Humphrey Bogart and Lauren Bacall talkin' dirty

THE BIG SLEEP, 1946

"She tried to sit on my lap while I was standing up."

Humphrey Bogart

THE BIG SLEEP, 1946

"It is easy to understand why the most beautiful poems about England in the spring were written by poets living in Italy at the time."

George Sanders to Gene Tierney
THE GHOST AND MRS. MUIR, 1947

"You know what I do with squealers? I let 'em have it in the belly so they can roll around for a long time thinking it over."

Richard Widmark to Mildred Dunnock
KISS OF DEATH, 1947

"King Solomon had the right idea about work. 'Whatever thy hand findeth to do,' Solomon said, 'do thy doggonedest.'"

William Powell to James Lydon
LIFE WITH FATHER, 1947

"Now, wait a minute, Susie. Just because every child can't get its wish, that doesn't mean there isn't a Santa Claus."

Edmund Gwenn to Natalie Wood
MIRACLE ON 34TH STREET, 1947

"Botchess? We ain' got no botchess! We don't need no botchess!! I don't haf to show dju any stinkin' botchess!!!"

Alfonso Bedoya blowing his cover

TREASURE OF THE SIERRA MADRE, 1948

“Nobody ever put anything over on Fred C. Dobbs.”

Humphrey Bogart

THE TREASURE OF THE SIERRA MADRE, 1948

“You’re the most beautiful plank in your husband’s platform.”

”That’s a heck of a thing to call a woman!”

Adolphe Menjou and Katharine Hepburn

STATE OF THE UNION, 1948

“One Rocco more or less isn’t worth dying for.”

Humphrey Bogart regarding Edward G. Robinson

KEY LARGO, 1948

“Look, I can understand the temptation of a young man over here–but a grandfather! Really, Colonel Plummer, you should have your brakes relined.”

Jean Arthur to Millard Mitchell

A FOREIGN AFFAIR, 1948

"You shoulda let 'em kill me 'cause I'm gonna kill you. I'll catch up with you! I don't know when, but I'll catch up with you. And every time you turn around, expect to see me, because one time you'll turn around and I'll be there. I'll kill you, Matt."

John Wayne to Montgomery Clift
RED RIVER, 1948

"I heard a scream, and I didn't know if it was me who screamed or not–if it was *I* or not."

Olivia De Havilland
THE SNAKE PIT, 1948

"I refuse to endanger the health of my children in a house with less than three bathrooms."

Myrna Loy to Melvyn Douglas
MR. BLANDINGS BUILDS HIS DREAM HOUSE, 1948

"What a dump!"

Bette Davis to Joseph Cotton
BEYOND THE FOREST, 1949

"In Italy for thirty years under the Borgias, they had warfare, terror, murder, bloodshed. They produced Michaelangelo, Leonardo da Vinci, and the Renaissance. In Switzerland they had brotherly love, five hundred years of democracy and peace, and what did they produce–the cuckoo clock!"

Orson Welles to Joseph Cotton
THE THIRD MAN, 1949

"What can I do, old man? I'm dead, aren't I?"
Orson Welles to Joseph Cotton
THE THIRD MAN, 1949

"Never apologize and never explain–it's a sign of weakness."
John Wayne's credo
SHE WORE A YELLOW RIBBON, 1949

"Made it, Ma!. . .Top of the world!"
Jimmy Cagney's dying words
WHITE HEAT, 1949

"A lot of guys make mistakes, I guess, but every one we make, a whole stack of chips goes with it. We make a mistake, and some guy don't walk away–forevermore, he don't walk away."
John Wayne to Forrest Tucker
SANDS OF IWO JIMA, 1949

"I suppose you know you have a wonderful body. I'd like to do it in clay."
Lola Albright to Kirk Douglas
CHAMPION, 1949

THE FIFTIES

"When it bleeds–the Red Sea!"
Jose Ferrer regarding his nose
CYRANO DE BERGERAC, 1950

"Fasten your seat belts we're in for a bumpy night."
Bette Davis to company
ALL ABOUT EVE, 1950

"Miss Caswell is an actress, a graduate of the Copacabana School of Dramatic Arts."
George Sanders to Bette Davis regarding Marilyn Monroe
ALL ABOUT EVE, 1950

"You're just not couth!"
Judy Holliday to Broderick Crawford
BORN YESTERDAY, 1950

"Crime is a left-handed form of human endeavour."
Sam Jaffe
THE ASPHALT JUNGLE, 1950

"I won't need that. He's a *young* lion."
Victor Mature to Hedy Lamarr
SAMSON AND DELILAH, 1950

"I've wrestled with reality for 35 years, and I'm happy, Doctor. I finally won out over it."

Jimmy Stewart to psychiatrist
HARVEY, 1950

"This floor used to be wood, but I had it changed. Valentino said, there's nothing like tile for the tango."

Gloria Swanson to William Holden
SUNSET BOULEVARD, 1950

"All right, Mr. DeMille, I'm ready for my closeup."

Gloria Swanson's fade out line
SUNSET BOULEVARD, 1950

"Pinch me, Rosie. Here we are, going down the river like Antony and Cleopatra on that barge!"

Humphrey Bogart to Katharine Hepburn
THE AFRICAN QUEEN, 1951

"If there's anything in the world I hate it's leeches–filthy little devils!!!"

Humphrey Bogart to Katharine Hepburn
THE AFRICAN QUEEN, 1951

"Nature, Mr. Allnut, is what we are put into this world to rise above."

Katharine Hepburn to Humphrey Bogart
THE AFRICAN QUEEN, 1951

"That's quite a dress you almost have on."
Gene Kelly to Nina Foch
AN AMERICAN IN PARIS, 1951

"Some people are better off dead–like your wife and my father, for instance."
Robert Walker to Farley Granger
STRANGERS ON A TRAIN, 1951

"I've met some hard boiled eggs, but you–you're twenty minutes!"
Jan Sterling to Kirk Douglas
ACE IN THE HOLE, 1951

"Tell Mama. Tell Mama all."
Elizabeth Taylor placating Montgomery Clift
A PLACE IN THE SUN, 1951

"Among the gods, your humor is unique."
Leo Genn's understatement to Peter Ustinov
QUO VADIS? 1951

"Hey, Stella!!. . .Hey, Stella!!!"
Marlon Brando fade out line
A STREETCAR NAMED DESIRE, 1951

"It's no good. I've got to go back. They're making me run. I've never run from anyone before."

Gary Cooper to Grace Kelly
HIGH NOON, 1952

"There's something about working the streets I like. It's the tramp in me, I suppose."
Charlie Chaplin to Claire Bloom
LIMELIGHT, 1952

"I believe that a man is fire and a woman fuel. And she who is born beautiful is born married."
Marlon Brando inscrutably wooing Jean Peters
VIVA ZAPATA, 1952

"I don't think Little Sheba's ever coming back, Doc. I ain't going to call her anymore."
Shirley Booth to Burt Lancaster
COME BACK LITTLE SHEBA, 1952

"A man's gotta dream; it comes with the territory."
Fredric March
DEATH OF A SALESMAN, 1952

"If we bring a little joy into your humdrum lives, it makes us feel our work ain't been in vain for nothin'."
Jean Hagen showing why she was best as a silent screen star
SINGIN' IN THE RAIN, 1952

"Only my friends call me 'wop'."
Frank Sinatra to Ernest Borgnine
FROM HERE TO ETERNITY, 1953

"There is a pain beyond pain, an agony so intense, it shocks the mind into instant beauty."
Vincent Price to Phyllis Kirk
HOUSE OF WAX, 1953

"Shane, come back. . .come back Shane!"
Brandon De Wilde's fade out line
SHANE, 1953

"What are you rebelling against?"

"What've you got?"
Marlon Brando, a rebel collecting causes
THE WILD ONE, 1953

"A kiss on the hand might feel very good, but a diamond tiara is forever."
Marilyn Monroe
GENTLEMEN PREFER BLONDES, 1953

"Prove it. . ."
Jack Palance's sinister refrain
SHANE, 1953

"Don't you think it's better for a girl to be preoccupied with sex than occupied?"

Maggie McNamara to David Niven
THE MOON IS BLUE, 1953

"Let me tell you what stooling is. Stooling is when you rat on your friends, the guys you're with."

Rod Steiger to Marlon Brando
ON THE WATERFRONT, 1954

"Tell me lies."

"I have waited for you, Johnny."

Sterling Hayden and Joan Crawford
JOHNNY GUITAR, 1954

"Ah, but the strawberries! That's–that's where I had them. They laughed and made jokes, but I proved beyond a shadow of a doubt, and with geometric logic, that a duplicate key to the wardroom icebox did exist."

Humphrey Bogart telling more than he intends to Jose Ferrer
THE CAINE MUTINY, 1954

"I could've been a contender. I could've had class and been somebody. Real class. Instead of a bum, let's face it, which is what I am. It was you, Charlie."

Marlon Brando to Rod Steiger

ON THE WATERFRONT, 1954

"I have a rendezvous with the Duchesse de Guermantes."

Ernest Thesiger

FATHER BROWN, 1954

"Just this once, Kirk, why don't you empty your own ashtrays?"

Edmond O'Brien to Warren Stevens

THE BAREFOOT CONTESSA, 1954

"Harry, we must beware of those men. They're desperate characters. . .Not one of them looked at my legs."

Jennifer Jones to Edward Underdown

BEAT THE DEVIL, 1954

"Yonda is duh castle of my fodda."

Tony Curtis in unmistakable Brooklynese

THE BLACK SHIELD OF FALWORTH, 1954

"Take back your mink from whence it came!"

Vivian Blaine to Frank Sinatra

GUYS AND DOLLS, 1955

"What do you feel like doing tonight?"

"I don't know, Ange. What do *you* feel like doing?"
Joe Montell and Ernest Borgnine's frequent refrain
MARTY, 1955

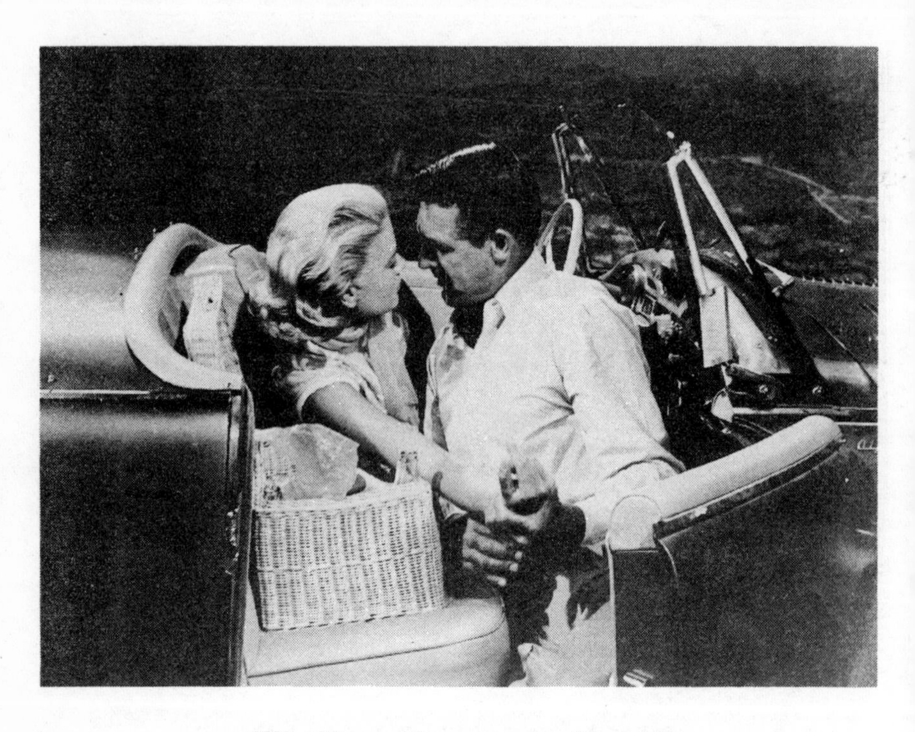

"Would you like a leg or a breast?"
Grace Kelly's picnic offer to Cary Grant
TO CATCH A THIEF, 1955

"Then the first thing that happens is I see you, and I thought this is going to be one terrific day so you better live it up, boy 'cause tomorrow you'll be nothing."

James Dean prophetic utterance to Natalie Wood

REBEL WITHOUT A CAUSE, 1955

"Whenever someone else is crying, I've gotta cry too. I'm sympathetic. I've got too much of a heart."

Burt Lancaster to Anna Magnani
THE ROSE TATTOO, 1955

"Man has a choice, and it's–the, the choice is what makes him a man,' see? You see, I do remember."

Jimmy Dean to Raymond Massey
EAST OF EDEN, 1955

"What seems to be the trouble, Captain?"

Mildred Natwick to Edmund Gwenn dragging a corpse
THE TROUBLE WITH HARRY, 1955

"Captain, it is I–Ensign Pulver–and I just threw your stinking palm tree overboard. Now, what's all this crud about no movie tonight?"

Jack Lemmon fade out line to Jimmy Cagney
MR. ROBERTS, 1955

"I wouldn't take you if you were covered in diamonds–upside down!"

Joan Crawford to Jeff Chandler
THE FEMALE ON THE BEACH, 1955

“We have not missed, you and I–we have not missed that many-splendored thing.”

William Holden to Jennifer Jones
LOVE IS A MANY-SPLENDORED THING, 1955

"Et cetera, et cetera, et cetera."
Yul Brynner frequent refrain
THE KING AND I, 1955

"I get so tired of just being told I'm pretty."
Kim Novak to William Holden
PICNIC, 1955

"I wanted to marry her when I saw the moonlight shining on the barrel of her father's shotgun."
Eddie Albert
OKLAHOMA!, 1955

"Moses, you stubborn, splendid, adorable fool!"
Anne Baxter to Charlton Heston
THE TEN COMMANDMENTS, 1956

"Years from now, when you talk about this–and you will–be kind."
Deborah Kerr to John Kerr
TEA AND SYMPATHY, 1956

"Oh, I see. . .the pellet with the poison's in the flagon with the dragon, the vessel with the pestle has the brew that is true."
Danny Kaye to Robert Middleton, trying to get it straight
THE COURT JESTER, 1956

"If thee talked as much to the Almighty as thee does to that horse, thee might stand more squarely in the light."

Dorothy McGuire to Gary Cooper

FRIENDLY PERSUASION, 1956

"He rises!"

Gregory Peck regarding the white whale

MOBY DICK, 1956

"The Tartar woman is for me, and my blood says, take her!"

John Wayne having his way with Susan Hayworth

THE CONQUEROR, 1956

"You give me powders, pills, baths, injections, and enemas–when all I need is love."

William Holden to Ann Sears

THE BRIDGE ON THE RIVER KWAI, 1957

"I know you have a civil tongue in your head–I sewed it there myself!"

Whit Bissell to his creation

I WAS A TEENAGE FRANKENSTEIN, 1957

"I'm not living with you. We occupy the same cage, that's all."
Elizabeth Taylor to Paul Newman
CAT ON A HOT TIN ROOF, 1958

"Life's never quite interesting enough, somehow. You people who come to the movies know that."

Shirley Booth to camera
THE MATCHMAKER, 1958

"A sculptor-friend of Auntie Mame's used this room for about six months. A divine man. Such talented fingers, but oh, what he did to my bust."

Rosalind Russell to Jan Handzlik
AUNTIE MAME, 1958

"It doesn't matter who gives them as long as you never wear anything second-rate. Wait for the first-class jewels, Gigi. Hold on to your ideals."

Isabel Jeans to Leslie Caron
GIGI, 1958

"Well, mustn't miss the old train, what, what? I must–I must stop saying 'What.' Cheeriebye. I must stop doing that too, I suppose."

David Niven to Wendy Hiller
SEPARATE TABLES, 1958

"Your eyes are full of hate, Forty-One. That's good. Hate keeps a man alive."

Jack Hawkins to Charlton Heston

BEN-HUR, 1959

"You don't understand, Osgood, I'm a man!"

"Well, nobody's perfect."

Jack Lemmon and Joe E. Brown's fade out lines

SOME LIKE IT HOT, 1959

"Darling, you're crying. I believe you're really sentimental after all."

Heather Sears misinterpreting Joe Lampton's tears

ROOM AT THE TOP, 1959

"In spite of everything, I still believe that people are good at heart."

Millie Perkins's last lines

THE DIARY OF ANNE FRANK, 1959

"Killers kill, squealers squeal."

Jean-Paul Belmondo to Jean Seberg

BREATHLESS, 1959

"You gentlemen aren't really trying to murder my son, are you?"

Jessie Royce Landis to hit-men

NORTH BY NORTHWEST, 1959

"Is your invitation to spread a little fertilizer still open?"

Gregory Peck wooing Ava Gardner

ON THE BEACH, 1959

THE SIXTIES

"Now, I may sound like a Bible-beater yellin' up a revival at a river-crossing camp-meeting, but that don't change the truth none."

John Wayne sweet-talking Linda Cristal
THE ALAMO, 1960

"Mother–what's the phrase?–isn't quite herself today."

Anthony Perkins to Janet Leigh
PSYCHO, 1960

"I love you, Spartacus."

Tony Curtis to Kirk Douglas
SPARTACUS, 1960

"Shut up and deal!"

Shirley MacLaine's fade out line to Jack Lemmon
THE APARTMENT, 1960

"Mama, face it: I was the slut of all time."

Elizabeth Taylor to Mildred Dunnock
BUTTERFIELD 8, 1960

"And what is love? Love is the mornin' and the evenin' star. . ."

Burt Lancaster's signature line

ELMER GANTRY, 1960

"Hello, Devil. Welcome to Hell."
Gene Kelly to Spencer Tracy
INHERIT THE WIND, 1960

"Eddie, you're a born loser."
George C. Scott to Paul Newman
THE HUSTLER, 1961

"This, then, is what we stand for: truth, justice and the value of a single human being."
Spencer Tracy to courtroom
JUDGMENT AT NUREMBERG, 1961

"Cross my heart and kiss my elbow."
Audrey Hepburn's frequent refrain
BREAKFAST AT TIFFANYS, 1961

"Just head for that big star straight on. The highway's under it, and it'll take us right home."
Clark Gable's last line on screen to Marilyn Monroe
THE MISFITS, 1961

"Fat man, you shoot a great game of pool."
Paul Newman to Jackie Gleason
THE HUSTLER, 1961

"Get up you scum suckin' pig!"

An enraged Marlon Brando to cowering desperado

ONE-EYED JACKS, 1961

"I'm not just talented. I'm geniused."

Rita Tushingham

A TASTE OF HONEY, 1961

"People who are very beautiful make their own laws."

Vivien Leigh to Warren Beatty

THE ROMAN SPRING OF MRS. STONE, 1961

"He's very progressive. He has all sorts of ideas about artificial insemination and all that sort of thing. He breeds all over the world."

Debbie Reynolds to Fred Astaire

THE PLEASURE OF HIS COMPANY, 1961

"Keep your pants on, Spartacus."

Capitalist Jimmy Cagney to Marxist Horst Buchholz

ONE, TWO, THREE, 1961

"He was a poet, a scholar and a mighty warrior. . .He was also the most shameless exhibitionist since Barnum and Bailey."

Arthur Kennedy eulogizing Peter O'Toole

LAWRENCE OF ARABIA, 1962

"Now look at me. I'm a bum. Look at me. Look at you. You're a bum. Look at you. And look at us. Look at us. C'mon, look at us. See? A couple of bums."

Jack Lemmon to Lee Remick

DAYS OF WINE AND ROSES, 1962

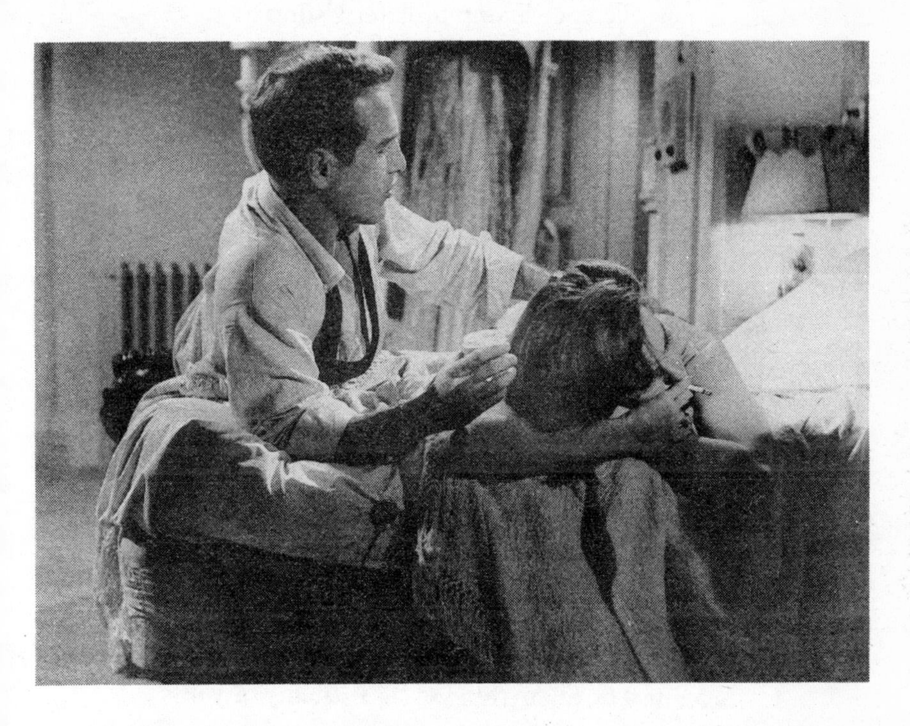

"I am not part of your luggage. Whatever I am, I am not part of your luggage."

Paul Newman to Geraldine Page
SWEET BIRD OF YOUTH, 1962

"God bless Captain Vere!"

Terence Stamp to Peter Ustinov

BILLY BUDD, 1962

"Obedience without understanding is a blindness too–is that all I wished on her?"

Anne Bancroft regarding her pupil, Patty Duke

THE MIRACLE WORKER, 1962

"Well, I suppose we'll have to feed the duchess. Even vultures have to eat."

Shirley MacLaine

THE CHILDREN'S HOUR, 1962

"That's my steak, Valance. Pick it up."

Jimmy Stewart to Lee Marvin

THE MAN WHO SHOT LIBERTY VALANCE, 1962

"Believe you me, if it didn't take men to make babies I wouldn't have anything to do with any of you!"

Gena Rowlands exasperated with the recalcitrant cowpoke Kirk Douglas

LONELY ARE THE BRAVE, 1962

"My name is Bond, James Bond."
Sean Connery's frequent refrain
JAMES BOND MOVIES, 1960s onward

"Boss, why did God give us hands? To grab. Well, grab!"
Anthony Quinn to Alan Bates
ZORBA THE GREEK, 1963

"Wake up, you country stewpot!. . .Rouse yourself from this pastoral torpor!"
Edith Evans to Hugh Griffith
TOM JONES, 1963

"Tom had always thought that any woman was better than none, while Molly never felt that one man was quite as good as two."
Michael MacLiammoir (narrator)
TOM JONES, 1963

"Better wed than dead!"
Steve McQueen proposing to Natalie Wood
LOVE WITH THE PROPER STRANGER, 1963

"Sometimes I wonder whose side God's on."
John Wayne in uncharacteristic moment of doubt
THE LONGEST DAY, 1963

"There has never been such a silence. . ."
Elizabeth Taylor regarding Richard Burton's death
CLEOPATRA, 1963

"The only question I ever ask any woman is: 'What time is your husband coming home?'"

Paul Newman to Patricia Neal

HUD, 1963

"Mr. President, I'm not saying we wouldn't get our hair mussed, but I do say not more than ten or twenty million killed tops, depending on the breaks."

George C. Scott to Peter Sellers

DR. STRANGELOVE OR HOW I LEARNED TO STOP WORRYING AND LOVE THE BOMB, 1964

"Where the devil are my slippers, Liza?"
Rex Harrison's last line to Audrey Hepburn
MY FAIR LADY, 1964

"At our last meeting, I died. It alters the appearance."
Deborah Kerr to Felix Aylmer
THE CHALK GARDEN, 1964

"He has every characteristic of a dog except loyalty."
Henry Fonda regarding Cliff Robertson
THE BEST MAN, 1964

"Do you accept the protection of this ignoble Caliban on any terms that Caliban cares to make, or is your. . .eh, *delicacy* so exorbitant that you would sacrifice a woman and her child to it?"
Rod Steiger offering escape for Julie Christie to a reluctant Omar Sharif
DR. ZHIVAGO, 1965

"There are worse things than chastity, Mr. Shannon."

"Yes–lunacy and death."

Deborah Kerr to Felix Aylmer

THE NIGHT OF THE IGUANA, 1964

"What happened?"

"Happened?. . .I didn't die. Everything that I loved was taken away from me and I did not die."

Rod Steiger trying to explain to Geraldine Fitzgerald
THE PAWNBROKER, 1965

"Your idea of fidelity is not having more than one man in bed at the same time."

Dirk Bogarde to Julie Christie
DARLING, 1965

"You dare to dicker with your pontiff?"

Rex Harrison to Charlton Heston
THE AGONY AND THE ECSTASY, 1965

"The world shall hear from me again. . ."

Christopher Lee
THE FACE OF FU MANCHU, 1965

"God always has another custard pie up His sleeve."

Lynn Redgrave
GEORGY GIRL, 1966

"My understanding of women goes only as far as the pleasures."

Michael Caine

ALFIE, 1966

"I swear, if you existed, I'd divorce you."
Elizabeth Taylor to Richard Burton
WHO'S AFRAID OF VIRGINIA WOOLF?,
1966

"Too bad it didn't happen further down the street–in front of the May Company. From *them*, you can collect! Couldn't you have dragged yourself another 20 feet?"

Walter Matthau giving legal counsel to Howard McNear

THE FORTUNE COOKIE, 1966

"Martha, will you show her where we keep the. . .er, euphemism?"

Richard Burton to Elizabeth Taylor regarding Sandy Dennis's trip to the. . .er, bathroom

WHO'S AFRAID OF VIRGINIA WOOLF?, 1966

"You know something, Virgil, you're the first person who's been around here to call. . .Nobody comes."

Rod Steiger to Sidney Poitier

IN THE HEAT OF THE NIGHT, 1967

"What we have here is a failure to communicate."

Strother Martin's sinister refrain to Paul Newman

COOL HAND LUKE, 1967

"What's the going price on integrity this week?"

Orson Welles to Oliver Reed

I'LL NEVER FORGET WHATSHISNAME, 1967

"Plastics!"

Walter Brooke's avuncular advice to Dustin Hoffman
THE GRADUATE, 1967

"Well, Tillie, when the hell are we going to get some dinner?"

Spencer Tracy's last line on film to Isabel Sanford
GUESS WHO'S COMING TO DINNER, 1967

"I feel like we've died and gone to heaven–only we had to climb up."

Mildred Natwick arriving breathless at Jane Fonda's fifth floor walk-up
BAREFOOT IN THE PARK, 1967

"She cut off her nipples with garden shears. You call that normal?"

Elizabeth Taylor to Brian Keith
REFLECTIONS IN A GOLDEN EYE, 1967

"We rob banks."

Warren Beatty and Faye Dunaway's cryptic job description
BONNIE AND CLYDE, 1967

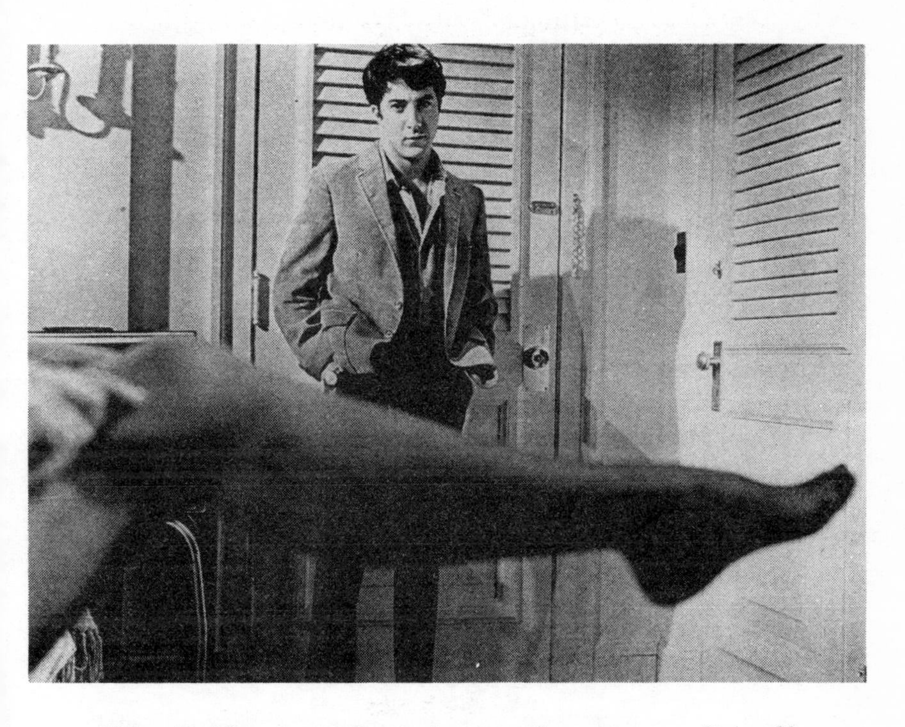

"Mrs. Robinson, you're trying to seduce me, aren't you?'
Dustin Hoffman to Anne Bancroft
THE GRADUATE, 1967

"Stop–Dave. Will-you-stop? I'm afraid. . .I'm-afraid, Dave. Dave. My-mind-is-going. . .I-can-feel-it. I-can-feel-it. . .There-is-no-question-about-it. . ."

Robot "Hal's" last line

2001: A SPACE ODYSSEY, 1968

"How could this happen? I was so careful. I picked the wrong play, the wrong director, the wrong cast–where did I go *right*?"

A desperate Zero Mostel to Gene Wilder

THE PRODUCERS, 1968

"Out here, due process is a bullet."

John Wayne exuding charm again

THE GREEN BERETS, 1968

"I told you 158 times I cannot stand little notes on my pillow. 'We are out of corn flakes. F.U.' It took me three hours to figure out F.U. was Felix Ungar. It's not your fault, Felix: it's a rotten combination, that's all."

Walter Matthau to Jack Lemmon

THE ODD COUPLE, 1968

"Oh, Andy–Andy or Jennie–I'm sorry my little darling, forgive me!"

Mia Farrow to her unborn child as she succumbs to the diabolists

ROSEMARY'S BABY, 1968

"Hello, gorgeous."
Barbra Streisand to her reflection in mirror
FUNNY GIRL, 1968

"How dear of you to let me out of jail."
Katharine Hepburn to Peter O'Toole
THE LION IN WINTER, 1968

"Well, I'll tell you the truth now. I ain't a real cowboy, but I am one helluvah stud."

Jon Voight
MIDNIGHT COWBOY, 1969

"Yowsir! Yowsir! Yowsir! Here they are again–these wonderful, wonderful kids, still struggling, still hoping as the clock of fate ticks away. The dance of destiny continues. The marathon goes on and on and on. How long can they last? Let's hear it. C'mon, let's hear it. Let's hear it."

Gig Young emceeing dance contest
THEY SHOOT HORSES DON'T THEY, 1969

"We've got to start thinking beyond our guns. Those days are closing fast."

William Holden to his gang
THE WILD BUNCH, 1969

"Nic, nic, nic, fire. . .Nic, nic, nic!"

Jack Nicholson's drinking refrain
EASY RIDER, 1969

"We blew it."

Peter (Captain America) Fonda to Dennis Hopper the night before they die
EASY RIDER, 1969

"Who *are* those guys?"
Robert Redford's frequent query to Paul Newman regarding the unshakable posse
BUTCH CASSIDY AND THE SUNDANCE KID 1969

"Fill your hand, you son of a bitch!"
John Wayne to Robert Duvall
TRUE GRIT, 1969

"Give me a girl at an impressionable age and she is mine for life."
Maggie Smith's credo
THE PRIME OF MISS JEAN BRODIE, 1969

"I used to–used to make obscene phone calls to her–collect–and she used to accept the charges all the time."
Woody Allen to Janet Margolin
TAKE THE MONEY AND RUN, 1969

"First we'll have an orgy, then we'll go see Tony Bennett."
Elliot Gould to Dyan Cannon, Robert Culp and Natalie Wood
BOB AND CAROL AND TED AND ALICE, 1969

THE SEVENTIES

"Does she smile when you mount her?"
Dustin Hoffman
LITLE BIG MAN, 1970

"Frank, were you on this religious kick at home, or did you crack up over here?"
Donald Sutherland to Robert Duvall
M*A*S*H, 1970

"Rommel, you beautiful bastard, I read your book."
George C. Scott regarding Karl Michel Vogler
PATTON, 1970

"It's not as easy getting laid as it used to be. I don't think I fuck more than a dozen new girls a year, now."
Jack Nicholson to Art Garfunkel
CARNAL KNOWLEDGE, 1971

"I know what you're thinking. Did he fire six shots or only five? Well, to tell you the truth, in all this excitement I've kinda lost track myself. But being this is a .44 magnum, the most powerful handgun in the world, and would blow your head clean off–you've got to ask yourself one question: do I feel lucky? Well, do ya, punk?"
Clint Eastwood to thug
DIRTY HARRY, 1971

"Men have paid $200 for me, and here you are, turning down a freebie. You could get a perfectly good dishwasher for that."

Jane Fonda to Donald Sutherland

KLUTE, 1971

"You've no right to call me to account. I've only come about my cough."

Peter Finch to camera
SUNDAY BLOODY SUNDAY, 1971

"You're greedy, unfeeling, inept, indifferent, self-inflating and unconscionably profitable. Aside from that, I have nothing against you. I'm sure you play a helluva game of golf."

George C. Scott to Richard Dysart
THE HOSPITAL, 1971

"If she was here I'd probably be just as crazy now as I was then in about five minutes–ain't that ridiculous? No it ain't really, 'cause being crazy about a woman like her is always the right thing to do."

Ben Johnson recalling Ellen Burstyn to Timothy Bottoms
THE LAST PICTURE SHOW, 1971

"I hate the beach. I hate the sun. I'm pale and I'm redheaded. I don't tan–I stroke!"

Woody Allen
PLAY IT AGAIN, SAM, 1972

"My father made him an offer he couldn't refuse."
Al Pacino to Diane Keaton
THE GODFATHER, 1972

"Lewis, what are we going to do, Lewis? You're the guy with the answers, what the hell do we do now?"

"Now you get to play the game."

Bert Reynolds telling Jon Voight what he doesn't want to hear
DELIVERANCE, 1972

"Screw Max!"

"I do!"

"So do I."

Michael York and Liza Minnelli regarding the bisexual Helmut Griem
CABARET, 1972

"How 'bout coming up to my place for a spot of heavy breathing?"

Walter Matthau to Carol Burnett
PETE 'N' TILLIE, 1972

"Live! Otherwise you got nothing to talk about in the locker room."

Ruth Gordon to Bud Cort
HAROLD AND MAUDE, 1972

“*Willkommen*, *bienvenue*, welcome.”
Joel Grey’s opening line
CABARET, 1972

"May I ask you a personal question: do you smile all the time?"

Barbra Streisand to Robert Redford
THE WAY WE WERE, 1973

"What would you like to have?"

"Sex."

George Segal asking Susan Anspach what she likes on restaurant menu
BLUME IN LOVE, 1973

"Was it in the nature of a serious offense? For example, was it in the nature of a felony or a misdemeanor?"

"Well, it was in the nature of shoplifting."

Jack Nicholson quizzing Randy Quaid
THE LAST DETAIL, 1973

"I'd only blow it."

Robert Redford's last line to Paul Newman regarding his share of the take
THE STING, 1973

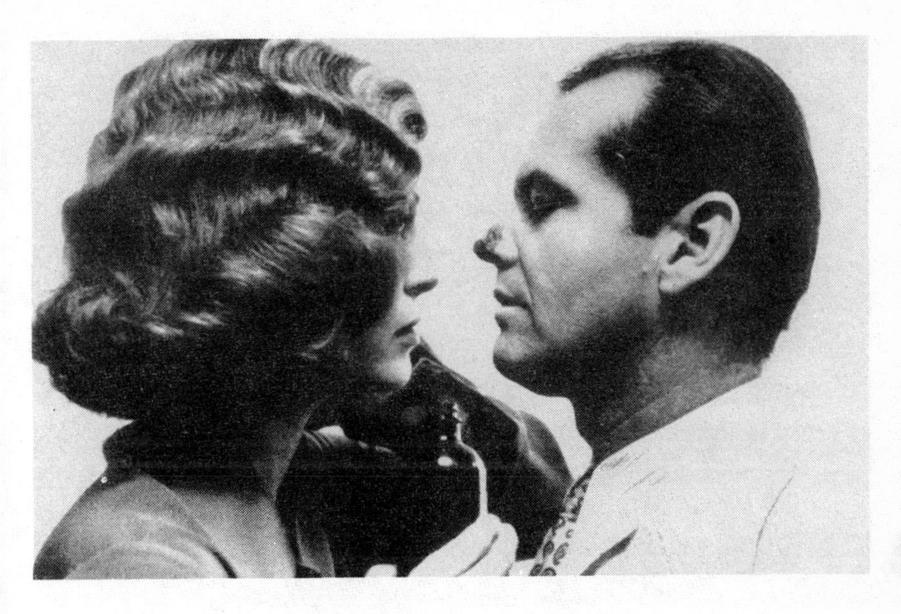

"He passed away two weeks ago and he bought the land a week ago. . .that's unusual."
Jack Nicholson to Faye Dunaway
CHINATOWN, 1974

"Want me to do your hair?"
Warren Beatty's codeword to Julie Christie
SHAMPOO, 1975

"Pardon me, boy, is this the Transylvania Station?"
Gene Wilder
YOUNG FRANKENSTEIN, 1974

"Hold it. . .the next man makes a move, the nigger gets it!"
Cleavon Little holding a gun to his own head
BLAZING SADDLES, 1974

"I wasn't popular at school on account of having no personality and not being pretty."
Sissy Spacek to Martin Sheen
BADLANDS, 1974

"Buried three of 'em. Good woman, bad diets."
Arthur Hunnicutt to Art Carney
HARRY AND TONTO, 1974

"I would be perfectly happy to have all my personal things burn up in a fire because I don't have anything personal–nothing of value. No, nothing personal except my *keys*, you see. . ."
Gene Hackman on phone to his intrusive landlady
THE CONVERSATION, 1974

"Peachy, I'm heartily ashamed for getting you killed instead of going home rich like you deserve to, on account of me being so bleedin' high and bloody mighty–can you forgive me?"

"That I can and that I do, Danny!"

Sean Connery and Michael Caine as they prepare to die

THE MAN WHO WOULD BE KING, 1975

"I don't wanna break up the meeting, or nothing, but she's something of a cunt, isn't she?"

Jack Nicholson regarding Louise Fletcher

ONE FLEW OVER THE CUCKOO'S NEST, 1975

"We need a bigger boat."

Roy Scheider to Robert Shaw on first sighting the shark

JAWS, 1975

"Just because you have good manners doesn't mean I suddenly turn into Dale Evans."

Ellen Burstyn to Kris Kristofferson

ALICE DOESN'T LIVE HERE ANYMORE, 1975

"I mean, they gonna kill you. They gonna tear your heart out if you keep on. They gonna walk on your soul, girl. . . .They gonna kill you in this town, girl."

Robert Dogul to Gwen Welles

NASHVILLE, 1975

"Kiss me, pig. . . .when I'm getting fucked I like to get kissed a lot."

Al Pacino regarding Charles Durning's attempts to con him

DOG DAY AFTERNOON, 1975

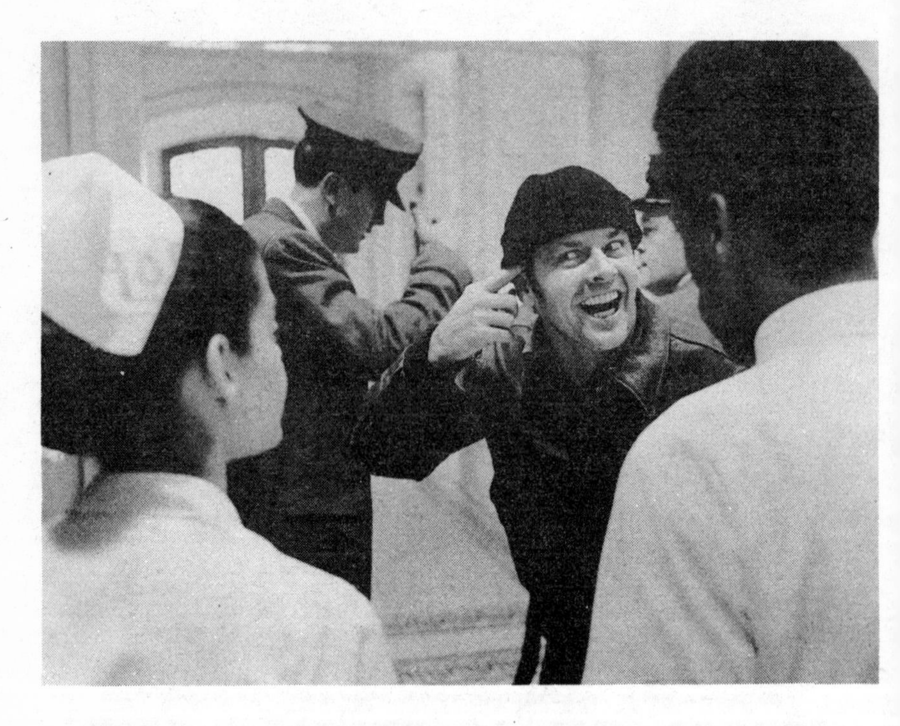

"They was giving me 10,000 watts a day, and, you know, I'm hot to trot. The next woman takes me out is going to light up like a pinball machine and pay off in silver dollars."

Jack Nicholson to other inmates

ONE FLEW OVER THE CUCKOO'S NEST, 1975

"I want all of you to get up out of your chairs. I want you to get up right now and go to the window, open it and stick your head out and yell, 'I'm as mad as hell, and I'm not going to take this anymore!'"

Peter Finch to TV viewers
NETWORK, 1976

"All the animals come out at night–poor skunk pussies, buggers, queens, fairies, dopers, junkies. . .sick, venial. . . some day a real rain will come and wash this scum off the streets."

Robert DeNiro to his diary
TAXI DRIVER, 1976

"I won't be wronged. I won't be insulted. I won't be laid a hand on. I don't do these things to others and I require the same of them."

John Wayne's last rallying cry
THE SHOOTIST, 1976

"I myself never surrendered. But they got my horse, and *it* surrendered."

Chief Dan George to Clint Eastwood
THE OUTLAW JOSEY WALES, 1976

"Hey, don't knock masturbation. It's sex with someone I love."

Woody Allen to Diane Keaton
ANNIE HALL, 1977

"Listen, I can't stand you, but you got a ten-year-old in there I'm nuts about. . ."

Richard Dreyfuss to Marsha Mason
THE GOODBYE GIRL, 1977

"May the Force be with you!"
Alec Quinness's mystical refrain
STAR WARS, 1977

"I made the seeds too big."

George Burns regarding avocados

OH, GOD!, 1977

"Let's discuss it over lunch."

Alan Bates to Jill Clayburgh

AN UNMARRIED WOMAN, 1978

"Why are you nervous? This isn't 'Have-a-gimp-over-for-dinner-night,' is it? You're not one of *those* weirdos."

Jon Voight to Jane Fonda

COMING HOME, 1978

"We can walk on the moon and turn garbage into roses."

"You're a poet!"

Paul Sorvino and Anne Ditchburn

SLOW DANCING IN THE BIG CITY, 1978

"Right turn, Clyde."

Clint Eastwood giving driving instructions to his chimpanzee

EVERY WHICH WAY BUT LOOSE, 1978

"You have to think about one shot. One shot is what it's all about. The deer has to be taken with one shot. I try to tell people that–they don't listen."

Robert DeNiro to Christopher Walken

THE DEER HUNTER, 1978

"I'm a zit, get it?"
John Belushi grossing out preppie types
ANIMAL HOUSE, 1978

"I like to watch."
Peter Sellers's ingenuous refrain
BEING THERE, 1979

"Whenever Mrs. Kissel breaks wind, we beat the dog."
Max Showalter to Dudley Moore regarding his housekeeper, Nedra Volz
"10", 1979

"Nobody made it. Nobody sold it. Nobody *sees* it. It doesn't exist.
Peter Boyle to George C. Scott regarding child porno flicks
HARDCORE, 1979

"Fun? How would you like to go around dressed like a head waiter for the last seven hundred years?"
George Hamilton complaining about being a vampire to Arte Johnson
LOVE AT FIRST BITE, 1979

"To be on the wire of life–the rest is waiting."
Roy Scheider to his Angel of Death, Jessica Lange
ALL THAT JAZZ, 1979

"You're just walkin' around to save funeral expenses."
Valerie Perrine to the down-and-out Robert Redford
THE ELECTRIC HORSEMAN, 1979

"I love the smell of napalm in the morning. . .it smells like victory."

Robert Duvall

APOCALYPSE NOW, 1979

"It's been a long time between offers. . .Kiss me: if that's all right, then everything else will be."

Sally Field responding to Beau Bridges's marriage proposal

NORMA RAE, 1979

"Does anybody have a valium?"

Charles Durning's frequent refrain

STARTING OVER, 1979

"Momma's boy, Momma's boy, I bet you're gonna cry. C'mon, Momma's boy, let's see you cry. C'mon, squirt a few. C'mon, cry! C'mon, cry! C'mon, c'mon, just a few. C'mon, squirt a few. C'mon, squirt. C'mon, cry! Cry! Cry! One-two-three, cry! C'mon, one-two-three, cry! C'mon, cry! C'mon, baby, c'mon little girl, cry. . .!"

Robert Duvall unmercifully taunting his son Michael O'Keefe

THE GREAT SANTINI, 1979

"I can feel it. . ."

Jack Lemmon's dying words to Jane Fonda regarding vibrations from nuclear reactor

THE CHINA SYNDROME, 1979

THE EIGHTIES

"C'mon. You're my brother. Be friends–ya fuckin' bum. Give me a break. C'mon, kiss me. Give me a kiss. C'mon."

Robert DeNiro's belated appeal to Joe Pesci
RAGING BULL, 1980

"We're on a mission from God."

John Belushi and Dan Aykroyd's frequent refrain
THE BLUES BROTHERS, 1980

"What I'm looking for is someone who can contribute to what England has given the world: culture, sophistication, genius–a little more than a hot dog, you know what I mean."

Mobster Bob Hoskins sharing his vision with Eddie Constantine and Stephen Davis
THE LONG GOOD FRIDAY, 1980

"Joey, have you ever been in a Turkish prison?"

Peter Graves's pederastic come-on to Rossie Harris
AIRPLANE!, 1980

"If God could do the tricks that we can do, He'd be a happy man."

Peter O'Toole to Steve Railsback regarding making movies
THE STUNT MAN, 1980

"He-e-e-re's Johnnie!"
Jack Nicholson to Shelley Duvall
THE SHINING, 1980

"I am not an animal!"
John Hurt
THE ELEPHANT MAN, 1980

"I think I'll take a bath."

"I'll alert the media."

Dudley Moore and Sir John Gielgud

ARTHUR, 1981

"Snakes. . .why does it always have to be snakes?"

Harrison Ford's Achilles' heel

RAIDERS OF THE LOST ARK, 1981

"You're not too bright. I like that in a man."

Kathleen Turner to William Hurt

BODY HEAT, 1981

"I believe God made me for a purpose. But he also made me fast. When I run, I feel His pleasure."

Ian Charleson's holy mission

CHARIOTS OF FIRE, 1981

"Are we having fun yet?"

Carol Burnett's oft-quoted line

FOUR SEASONS, 1981

"Ya wanna dance or would you rather just suck face?"
Henry Fonda's octogenarian raunch to Katharine Hepburn
ON GOLDEN POND, 1981

"*Ze* soldiers are very *hoppy* shooting *ze pipples* who say that *ze pipples* are not *hoppy*."

George Hamilton laying it on thick

ZORRO, THE GAY BLADE, 1981

"It's amazing what you can do with a cheap piece of meat if you know how to treat it."
Paul Bartel regarding the unidentified dish he is serving
EATING RAOUL, 1982

"There's nothing more inconvenient than an old queen with a head cold."
Robert Preston to Julie Andrews
VICTOR/VICTORIA, 1982

"Live? I can't go on *live*!! I'm a movie star–not an actor!"
Peter O'Toole to Mark Linn-Baker
MY FAVORITE YEAR, 1982

"The only reason you're still living is that I never kissed you."
Charles Durning to Dustin Hoffman
TOOTSIE, 1982

"I used to have to fake orgasm during masturbation."
The newly liberated Andrea Martin to Saul Rubinex.
SOUP FOR ONE, 1982

"E.T. phone home."
E.T.'s tearful refrain
E.T.–THE EXTRA-TERRESTRIAL, 1982

"Go ahead, make my day."
Clint Eastwood talking trash to punk
SUDDEN IMPACT, 1983

"See, I never trust happiness. . .I never did, I never will."

Robert Duvall to Tess Harper

TENDER MERCIES, 1983

"Tomorrow you'll know I wasn't kidding and you'll think I was crazy, but look, I figure it this way: better to be king for a night than schmuck for a lifetime."

Robert (Rupert Pupkin) DeNiro to T.V. audience

THE KING OF COMEDY, 1983

"We all have our little sorrows, Ducky. You're not the only one. The littler you are, the larger the sorrow. You think you loved him?. . .What about *me*!"

Tom Courtenay to Zena Walker regarding Albert Finney's demise

THE DRESSER, 1983

"We came, we saw, we kicked its ass!"

Bill Murray to spectators regarding expulsion of ghost

GHOSTBUSTERS, 1984

"Tell Victor that Ramon–the fella he met about a week ago–tell him that Ramon went to the clinic today and I found out that I had. . .eh, herpy simplex ten, and I think Victor should go check himself out with his physician to make sure everything is fine before things start falling off the man."

"Perhaps you should tell him that."

Eddie Murphy gaining entrance to exclusive club

BEVERLY HILLS COP, 1984

"I can't believe I gave my panties to a geek."
Molly Ringwald about Anthony Michael Hall
SIXTEEN CANDLES, 1984

"I mean. . .what do they (women) do, *together*?"

"Well, they use their tongues, foreign implements, eventually reach orgasm, and they quarrel about the condition of the room, and go out to a French movie. It's what makes them happy."
Psychologist Bob Ellis explaining to Norman Kaye how "they" do "it"
MAN OF FLOWERS, 1984

"But why. . .why would God choose an obscene child to be his instrument?"
F. Murray Abraham's obsession regarding the impetuous Mozart, Tom Hulce
AMADEUS, 1984

"Just a few things I like to get straight, right up front, so that there's no misunderstandings later on. I do not do animal acts. I do not do S and M or any variations on that particular bent. No water sports either. I will not shave my pussy. No fist-fucking, and absolutely no coming in my face."
Melanie Griffith laying down a few ground rules to Craig Wasson
BODY DOUBLE, 1984

"I'll be back. . ."
Arnold Schwartzenegger
THE TERMINATOR, 1984

"Come on, Chawley. Ya wanna do it? Let's do it, right here on the Oriental."

Anjelica Huston to Jack Nicholson

PRIZZI'S HONOR, 1985

"I used to sit on our front gallery every morning and every evening just to nod hello to Roy John Murray."

Geraldine Page reminiscing to Rebecca DeMornay

THE TRIP TO BOUNTIFUL, 1985

"I've seen the future! It's a bald headed man from New York!"

Albert Brooks suffering from Yuppie hysteria

LOST IN AMERICA, 1985

"You know, if you shoot me you'll lose a lot of these humanitarian awards."

Chevy Chase to police chief

FLETCH, 1985

"If this is foreplay, I'm a dead man!"

Steve Guttenberg to the seductive alien Tahnee Welch

COCOON, 1985

"I wanna be just like you. . .all I need is a lobotomy and some tights."

Judd Nelson to varsity wrestler Emilio Estevez
THE BREAKFAST CLUB, 1985

"It's just a romance, but it's *so* beautiful."
William Hurt to Raul Julia regarding *his* version of *his* movie
KISS OF THE SPIDER WOMAN, 1985

"You should have asked permission."

"I did. She said yes."

Klaus-Maria Brandauer and Robert Redford in classic exchange regarding Meryl Streep

OUT OF AFRICA, 1985

"Did you ever need someone?"

"All the time."

Cathy Tyson and Bob Hoskins talking at cross purposes

MONA LISA, 1986

"Cameron's so tight if you stuck a piece of coal up his ass in two weeks you'd have a diamond."

Matthew Broderick to camera

FERRIS BUELLER'S DAY OFF, 1986

"Why did you put your head in the oven?"

"Oh, I don't know, Meg. . . .I'm havin' a bad day–it's been a real bad day."

Sissy Spacek explaining her suicide attempt to Jessica Lange

CRIMES OF THE HEART, 1986

"Feed me Seymour. . .feed me all night long."

Plant (Levi Stubb's voice) to Rick Moranis

LITTLE SHOP OF HORRORS, 1986

"I'll send you a love letter straight from my heart, fucker. You know what a love letter is? It's a bullet from a fucking gun, fucker. You receive a love letter from me, you're fucked forever. You understand, fuck? I'll send you straight to hell, fucker!"

Dennis Hopper's Fugue in F to Kyle MacLachan

BLUE VELVET, 1986

"Get away from her, you *bitch*!"

Sigourney Weaver to alien queen regarding the orphan

ALIENS, 1986

"Peggy, you know what a penis is–stay away from it."

Barbara Harris giving motherly advice to Kathleen Turner

PEGGY SUE GOT MARRIED, 1986

"They're ba-ack!"

Heather O'Rourke's ominous announcement

POLTERGEIST II: THE OTHER SIDE, 1986

"I'll be takin' these Huggies and. . .uh, whatever cash you got."

Nicholas Cage holding up convenience store in dual role of father and hood

RAISING ARIZONA, 1987

"Greed is good! Greed is right! Greed works! Greed will save the U.S.A.!"

Michael Douglas sounding Yuppie credo to stockholders

WALL STREET, 1987

"Just one thing. I don't never wanna fall in love. I don't want to go through that again."

"Hey, don't worry, nobody's ever loved me yet."

Faye Dunaway and Mickey Rourke falling in love

BARFLY, 1987

"I see your schwartz is as big as mine. Now let's see how well you handle it."

Rick Moranis to Bill Pullman regarding their light-sabers

SPACEBALLS, 1987

"Except for socially, you're my role model."

Joan Cusack to Holly Hunter

BROADCAST NEWS, 1987

"I *won't* be ignored!"
Glenn Close's ominous warning to Michael Douglas
FATAL ATTRACTION, 1987

"That bitch! She thinks her shit don't stink."
Mercedes Ruehl regarding Michelle Pfeiffer
MARRIED TO THE MOB, 1988

"It's the only game where a black man can wave a stick at a white man without starting a riot."
Gene Hackman to Willem Dafoe regarding baseball
MISSISSIPPI BURNING, 1988

"I really like you Tomas. You are the complete opposite of kitsch. In the Kingdom of Kitsch, you would be a monster."
Lena Olin to Daniel Day-Lewis
THE UNBEARABLE LIGHTNESS OF BEING, 1988

"K-Mart sucks!"
Dustin Hoffman putting it all together
RAIN MAN, 1988

"Sometimes I sing and dance around my house in my underwear. That doesn't make me Madonna."
Joan Cusack to Melanie Griffith
WORKING GIRL, 1988

"This is the damndest season I ever seen: the Durham Bulls can't lose and I can't get laid."

Susan Sarandon to herself
BULL DURHAM, 1988

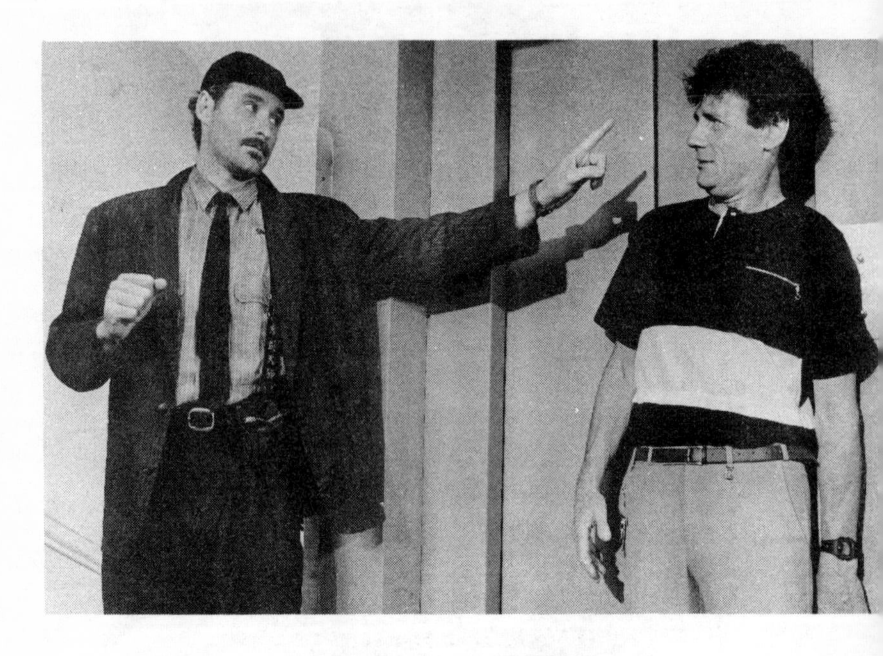

"Don't call me stupid!"
Kevin Kline's frequent refrain
A FISH CALLED WANDA, 1988

"I've distilled everything to one simple principle–win or die!"

Glenn Close to John Malkovich

DANGEROUS LIAISONS, 1988

"Phone call from God. . .if it had been collect, it would have been daring."

Robin Williams to Gale Hansen

DEAD POET'S SOCIETY, 1989

"We had a town once, Charlie. . .had a mother and father. . . things, things that made sense. Do you remember the things that made sense? Things you could count on? Before we all got so lost? What are we gonna do, Charlie? What am I gonna do, man?"

The disabled Tom Cruise lying on Mexican roadside with Willem Dafoe

BORN ON THE FOURTH OF JULY, 1989

"Hey, is this Heaven?"

"No, it's Iowa."

Ray Liotta (Shoeless Joe) to Kevin Costner

FIELD OF DREAMS, 1989

"I went on a long-range patrol, Sir. And we kidnapped a girl from a village. And the other four men raped her, and they murdered her. And I failed, Sir, to stop them."

A shattered Michael J. Fox to army chaplain, Sam Robards

CASUALTIES OF WAR, 1989

"I'll have what she's having."
Estelle Reiner to waiter after watching Meg Ryan's fake orgasm at nearby table
WHEN HARRY MET SALLY, 1989

"It only took me six days. . .same time it took the Lord to make the world."
Morgan Freeman to Dan Aykroyd regarding driving Jessica Tandy to the Piggly-Wiggly
DRIVING MISS DAISY, 1989

"Have you ever danced with the devil in the pale moonlight?"
Jack Nicholson's diabolical refrain
BATMAN, 1989

THE NINETIES

"You know what your problem is, Joey? You're a pig. And you're a chauvinist. And you have no respect for women."

"Oh. . .well I guess dinner and a blow job is out of the question then, huh?"

Robin Williams wooing Judith Hoag
CADILLAC MAN, 1990

"Did I ever tell you that this here jacket represents a symbol of my individuality and my belief in personal freedom?"

Nicholas Cage's frequent refrain regarding his beloved snake-skin jacket
WILD AT HEART, 1990

"Now you know how to do this, right? You got to remember to put one in his brain. Your first shot puts him down; then you put one in his brain; then he's dead; then we go home."

Al Mancini to Gabriel Byrne on "wacking" John Turturro
MILLER'S CROSSING, 1990

"Try the cock, Albert. It's a delicacy, and you know where it's been."

Helen Mirren to gourmand Michael Gambon
THE COOK, THE THIEF, HIS WIFE, AND HER LOVER, 1990

"I love you, Molly. I've always loved you."
"Ditto."

Patrick Swayze and Demi Moore
GHOST, 1990

"Go back. . .go back. . .go back. . .leave him alone. . .go back!"

Richard Harris beating back the waves from the corpse of his son, Sean Bean

THE FIELD, 1990

"If you can't trust your mother, who can you trust?"

John Cusack regarding the homicidal Anjelica Huston

THE GRIFTERS, 1990

"I have to go now. I'm having an old friend for dinner."

Anthony (Hannibal the Cannibal) Hopkins's fade out line to Jodie Foster regarding his next victim

SILENCE OF THE LAMBS, 1990